I0782686

Questions For Content

Thom Lancaster

http://thomlancaster.com

About This Book

The information in this book was originally conceived to be presented as a video training seminar. The resulting training has been reshaped and rewritten into its current format.

The training is designed to show how online question and answer sites can be used to produce high quality content for areas. The resulting content can be used to populate websites and the results can also be distributed as information products.

Dedication

This book is dedicated to everyone who has supported my on my Internet Marketing journey so far. You have my grateful thanks the faith that you've shown in me and towards my products.

I hope that I can provide just as much support for your own online explorations and that they bring with them both success and fulfilment.

Questions For Content

Thom Lancaster

http://thomlancaster.com

Table of Contents

Table of Figures

About The Author

Thom Lancaster is a UK based Internet Marketer. He has particular interests in the generation of quality content to use online and in creating information products. Thom has been researching and releasing information products online since 2009. He has developed systematic processes that can be used to create high quality products.

You can find out more about Thom's activities, as well as read and comment on his latest blog posts at http://thomlancaster.com.

Chapter 1 - Introduction

About *Questions For Content*

As an online marketer, content creation should be an important aspect of your business. It is certainly important for mine.

You can never have too much content. Content is needed to keep your websites fresh and to keep visitors returning to read new articles and blog posts. You need content to build up valuable information products which you can give away or sell. You can always produce content in advance of when it's needed as well. If you do product content carefully, it need not date.

I created this book, as I know that many marketers find it difficult to create content. They don't know what to write about, how to structure their content or how to find the information necessary to compile the content and keep this of high value.

In *Questions For Content*, I'm going to share with you one of the processes I use to create quality content. It's a process I can even use in areas where I don't have a great level of expertise.

You can apply these same techniques to your own niche and your own business.

It all comes down to one underlying principle. This is using question sites in the right manner. This is a way that's very different to the techniques that other marketers will teach you.

I also want to throw in a few more valuable hints and tips as you go through your *Questions For Content* journey.

A First Look At Question Sites

Did you know that there are many sites on the Internet that contain all the information that you need to produce fresh content for your websites, your blogs and your information products? Further, people are willingly adding new information to those sites all the time, ready to be reshaped into content. This means that the ideas that are presented are fresh and wide-ranging.

These sites are question and answer sites. The type of sites where one person puts up a question and a variety of people respond with their answers, advice and ideas. It's a form of crowdsourcing. It's great for these sites as they're generating their own content and not having to put the effort in to write questions and to keep the site active. There also tends to be a good community feel on these sites, so these contributors continue to stay involved with the question and answer sites for the long-term.

This book, *Questions For Content*, is designed to show you how you can use question and answer sites on the Internet the right way. That's by using these sites as the basis for producing high quality original content for your own business needs. That word original is important, as what you can never do is to just take what other people have written on the sites and *"copy and paste"* that content. That approach wouldn't be correct. But, what you can do is use the answers that the site contributors have provided to help you to explore ideas and to provide you with inspiration for your own content. That's the whole basis of this book.

The *Questions For Content* Syllabus

This book is split into six chapters, to take you through everything from understanding content and the specific question site that I recommend, to seeing a case study of content creation and finishing with an action plan to develop content that's relevant for you.

Chapter 1, which is the chapter that you're looking at now, introduces the book and runs through what you can expect to find inside it.

Chapter 2 looks at content in more detail. In Chapter 2, I'm going to more formally explore with you what the word "*content*" means on the Internet and why it's both important and necessary for you as a basis for your own sites and your own blogs. You need to appreciate that you can't really exist without having content available as a marketer.

Chapter 3 focuses more specifically on question sites. I'm going to share some examples of question and answer sites, focusing on one of these in particular which I think represents the best use of your time. Of course, this chapter will be linked back to solving the problem of content creation.

Chapter 4 is where we really hit the meat of the book. I've identified seven different ways in which you can use question sites to help with your content creation. I tend to focus in on one of these ways in particular, but I do like you to have plenty of options available to you.

In **Chapter 5**, I'm going to show you, start to finish, how to put the many ideas of the book together to create content. I show you a case study of how you can use the information found on a question site and use that to create an original and engaging piece of content that will interest your site visitors. I even suggest several different ways in which you can present the information to generate content in different styles.

The final chapter is **Chapter 6**. Rather than just a summary, I'm focusing this last chapter on the positive actions you can take to have success with the methods that you've found inside *Questions For Content*.

This is very much a book that works best when you put the information provided into action. As you read, I recommend that you explore the sites mentioned and think about what type of content will work best for your own business. By all means pause your reading at any time and start to generate your own content.

I've created this book to provide you with actionable techniques. I really want you to get the most you to benefit as much as possible from my experience.

Let's get started properly and discover how we should really be thinking about content.

Questions For Content

Chapter 2 – How Should You Be Thinking About Content And Why Is It So Important For Your Business?

What Is Content?

It's important to start this chapter by defining content and what this means for us as marketers.

You can think of content as existing in many different online marketing scenarios, but for me, the easiest way to think about this is as the substance you have on your website. Once you separate off how the website works, or the ways in which you make the site look pretty, the content is what you have left.

The content is what your visitors will focus in on once they arrive at the site. Nowadays, most content gets found by a visitor clicking on a link from another site, following a social media recommendation or being referred through a Google search. The quality of the content is what keeps your visitor engaged with your site and encourages them to interact with you, join your mailing list or click on one of the adverts that stands to earn you money.

You'll give visitors a good first impression if there are several visible pieces of content on your site. To give you a few examples, a standard type of content they might expect to find would be articles, usually a few hundred words long. You might be displaying shorter blog posts longer guides providing more thorough solutions to problems. Many sites focus on the latest news in their niche or in providing commentary to external events. They're all examples of different types of content that might work for you

Another type of content which is very popular, particularly for affiliate marketing sites, is to use a review based format. Many reviews on the Internet aren't as unbiased as visitors would like to believe. This is because these reviews might provide links to where a certain item can be purchased from. By adding affiliate links, you can earn money from the sales that you refer.

A further way of presenting content that I use all the time is in the format of video. From the view of building up your own content, this is an interesting one as I place most of my videos on YouTube. You don't just need to generate content for sites that you own, but also those larger commercial sites and social media properties on which you want to have some form of presence. Now, in the case of YouTube, you can also embed the results on your own sites, so using video creation as part of your content generation strategy can benefit you in multiple ways.

Images are also a popular way in which to present content. People like to look as photos and pictures and they like to share funny memes. You can present data in the form of an infographic. Further, this is all far from an exhaustive list. It's just there to give you a flavour of some of the different types of content that you might want to create as you grow your business.

To make this book easy to understand, I'm focus the examples on creating web content. But this same process can also be used if you create other types of content with your name attached on it. You could expand this strategy and generate information products. You could use the information to write a Kindle book. You can even take some of the hints that you discover and use them as the basis for tweets or other social media messages.

Similarly, the examples are also focused on written content, particularly that suitable for shorter articles or for blog posts. But that's just one modality which you can use to present information. If you do like creating videos, just generate the knowledge you need using the methods that I outline, but record a video instead of creating a written post. If you like to talk, you might use a podcast as your preferred communication medium. Everything is intended to be flexible and to be applicable in the manner that is most suitable for you.

What Is Good Content?

The previous section has provided you with a high level overview of how content works with online marketing strategies. But not all content is created equally.

I want to help you to change your mindset about content away from just putting up a lot of low value text to fill blank space on one of your sites. I want you to start thinking about valuing high quality content.

To put it simply, this high quality content is what makes visitors want to stay on your website.

When somebody clicks through to visit your site, they tend to make a split second decision. If your site is packed full of adverts and if that person can't find what they want, then that visitor will not consider your site to be very good. They'll go somewhere else. If you're a store selling your own products then that's bad news for you. That visitor is going to go and check out one of your competitors instead.

Even if you just want to engage people and interest them in one of your own hobbies or interests, you still want this high quality type of content there. It needs to be very attractive to your target audience. If they've clicked through expecting to see an article on how to train their poodle then that's what should be there. This could perhaps be supported by appropriate pictures and maybe even a video tutorial, but generally there should be something that answers the question that that visitor had when they clicked through to your site.

Creating good content will help you to build a relationship with your visitors and with your customers. It means that people will go back to your site again and again because they will value the high quality content that you're provided to them. They may sign up to your email mailing list. Most importantly, they're going to be getting something which is valuable to them. As a result having high quality content should be something that you consider to be of real importance.

I want to also add the message that in my mind, good content should be original to you. You should really have a unique angle to how you present your content. But, even if you find that a standard method of presentation works for your area, you still need to make sure that the same content isn't repeated across multiple sites. Chances are that your visitor will be visiting multiple sites in your field or they may already be familiar with your competitors. If they keep coming across the same content, they'll assume that you haven't created it.

They'll probably assume that it's not even very good. They may not want to visit your site again.

You also shouldn't be trying to game Google. I know that marketers put out information products all the time claiming that they know the latest Google loophole designed to get you high search engine rankings.

That just isn't a long term solution.

Google is very clever with its algorithms and it can identify the sites that visitors like and those that they don't like. If they refer a visitor to your site and that same visitor is back searching just seconds later, it probably means that they didn't think that your content was of good quality or relevant. Over time, Google can factor that into its search algorithms so that it sends visitors to site that are generally seen as satisfying visitors. That's another place where having original content also really helps. Having all that good content helps people to stick with your site. We want people to stay with you for as long as possible.

Now, there are occasional ways you can duplicate your own content. For instance, if you take a video, you host it on YouTube and then you embed that video in your site then that's generally okay. Google's quite happy with that because you're making use of one of the site services that they provide.

But even so, if somebody searches for that topic, are they going to find the Google site, the YouTube site with the video on, or are they going to find your website? Really, to find your website, you're going to want accompanying textual content so that there's something more than purely going to YouTube. You may still need to match things up a bit.

There's also a principle which says that if you produce high quality content then people will go out of their way to share it with their friends. This might mean they post a link from their own site or from their own blog, but more often nowadays it means that people want to share this using social media. They'll tweet about your content. They may put a post on Facebook and tell their friends about it. But they will be helping to promote more videos and more content for you.

That's what is called a *"viral effect"*. A good piece of content will be widely spread and it will bring more and more people to your site. That's great for you because they can then take advantage of any offers you make on your site besides the content. They can sign up for your mailing list. They can click on your adverts. You've got those people interested because they know you're providing a high quality service.

Properties Of Good Content

There are five properties that I think of as personifying good and high quality content.

The content you produce needs to be:

- Original

- Unique

- Interesting

- Engaging

- Inspiring

Google values **original** content. That means that it's not available elsewhere. It definitely shouldn't be taken word for word from another source.

Content needs to be **unique** so it's something that gives you something distinctive about your site. If you can be addressing a topic that other marketers in your niche are missing, you have an immediate advantage over them.

Questions For Content

Content should be **interesting** because people just get turned off by boring and uninteresting content. Even when this is on a unique area, then it won't hold the appeal to your visitors. They will click back away from your site.

By the same token, content should be **engaging** for your visitors. If you've got a blog then you want to try and get people to leave comments. This shows that they're interested and they want to find out more. It will even give you a bonus of offering you more ideas for producing content in the future.

I like the word **inspiring** because something that encourages people to take action on what they've read immediately demonstrates real value. On a page about poodle training, an appropriate action might be if your visitor tries out a technique and then provides a comment about what they've done. An alternative action might be for them to buy your book about dog training.

All these five properties fit together to show that you're producing and providing good content.

Working Around The Timing Pressures Posed By Good Content

I've already touched on this in Chapter 1, but to close this chapter, I want to reiterate that there are challenges posed when you want to ensure that all your content is good.

Like so many things in life, the biggest challenge, simply, is time. There are only so many hours in the day and regardless of how smart you work, you can never go beyond 24 hours in a day because it just becomes an impossibility of physics.

If you want good content, it's going to take you much more time to write well. You really need good levels of organisation if you want to avoid just putting any old rubbish online. That may just not be inspiring and may hurt you in the long run. Once you put content up there, it tends to be around forever, unless you make a real effort to get rid of it.

You may also want to think about good content being very timely and topical. For instance, one method often used to create blog posts is to provide comments on the news. For example, if you run a site related to technology then providing your own commentary on the technology news can be an excellent way to do this. But these posts can date quite quickly and the whole news area can go out of fashion unless you're able to produce that content as and when it's needed. That just adds to the time pressures.

Now, a completely alternative strategy is to try and produce evergreen content that won't go out of date. There are a lot of niches where this works quite well. For instance, going back to training poodles, chances are that those methods will not change greatly, so evergreen content of quality can be a good time saver. You do still need to consider a certain set of poodle owners who are looking for new methods to replace the ones they've tried which don't seem to work so well for them.

If you can produce evergreen content and can find inspiring ideas then this can be valuable in the long term. But it's going to be hard to come up with those ideas. I use one technique which is to keep a notepad full of ideas for my own sites and blogs and go through them, but even so that's all about being organised. If you just decide *"I need to produce content today"* then working without a good set of ideas of value, you have to have different solutions available to you.

That's where I feel question and answer sites best come in, which is the subject of Chapter 3.

Questions For Content

Chapter 3 – A Closer Look At The Question Site Solution For Your Content Needs

The Simple Solution For Content Generation

What then is the simple solution if you need to generate new content for online sites.

It's the one that this book has been geared towards. That's to use Question and Answer sites.

These sites are places on the Web where groups of people gather together and generally, somebody will post a question. It's something they need answering. It may be very trivial, it may be something where the answer is all over the Web, but the kind of people who use question and answer sites don't always want to search that far.

Questions For Content

There can also be some very challenging questions posted where people do want expert opinion. It's by the sharing of expert opinion and collecting together the views from multiple different people that the original question poster can come up with what they feel is a balanced answer. Often on these sites, of course, somebody may be quite happy to post a set of questions themselves but also to participate and answer other people's questions as well.

Example Question and Answer Sites

There are many sites of this type on the Web and I'm not going to attempt to list them all for the purpose of the **Questions For Content** book. I'm going to focus on two in particular, one of which is Yahoo! Answers, which is one of the longest lasting question sites. It's gone through changes of names. There's also a more recent site called Quora which is one that I tend to go through first because of the high level of expertise displayed by many of the people who post on there.

I'll use Quora for most of the examples in the book, but first I want to show you what Yahoo! Answers looks like. You can see Yahoo! Answers in Figure 1.

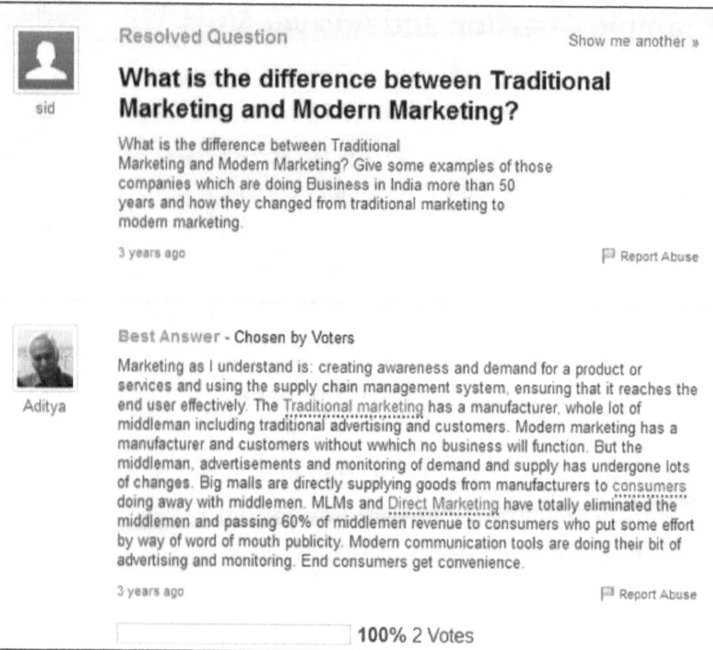

Figure 1 - Sample Question on Yahoo! Answers

In the case of Figure 1, somebody has posted the question *"What is the different between traditional marketing and modern marketing?"* and they go into a bit of detail about the question. There are various answers that have been given to that and Yahoo! provides the best answer first because that's the one that most people have said is important. This is just really a short description which factually answers that question.

Now, one useful thing about Yahoo! Answers is that questions are visible to the public by default so the information you need is there without you needing to set up an account or register if all you want to do is to read existing answers. Answers often appear in search engine results in Google which means you can find them.

I find Quora to be a much more developed site. It's not been around for as long as Yahoo! Answers and to get the best out of Quora, you need to be logged in. I think you're limited to reading one question at a time in a certain time period if you're not logged in but there's a very quick sign-up process. You can do this using Facebook Connect or you can set up a different account if you prefer to keep your social media accounts separate to one another.

Figure 2 is an example of a question being asked on Quora.

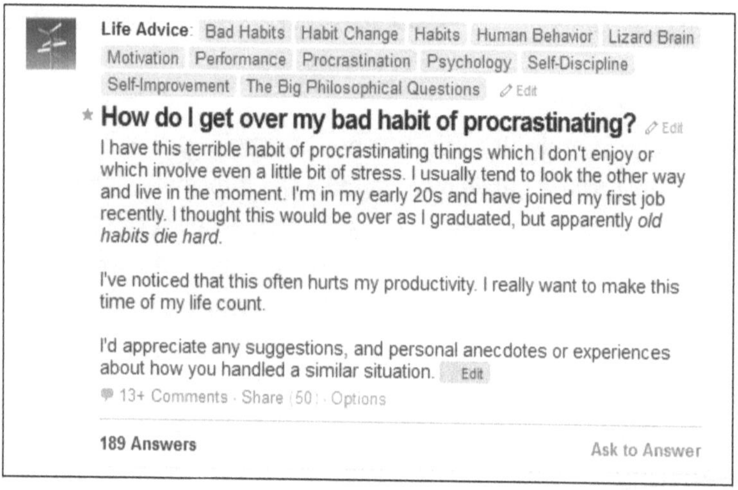

Figure 2 - Sample Question on Quora

Figure 2 shows a really typical type of question. *"How do I get over my bad habit of procrastinating?"* You can see it's been tagged by all sorts of different tags such as *"bad habits"*, *"habit change"*, *"human behaviour"*, *"self-discipline"*. As a member, you can add your own tags which helps to make these findable once you're on the site. Towards the bottom, you'll see this has received 13 comments and 189 answers. So a lot of people are interested in providing answers for this.

You can also provide answers yourself and clearly, with 189 answers, there's no chance that I could show you them all. But the users of Quora can vote answers up and down. There's an up arrow and a down arrow to choose which the best solutions are and that means that this is community-monitored and the most useful answers will be at the top.

When you're using Quora for research, that also means that you just need to look really at the first few answers to get what are the most popular views and you may want to look at a selection of later answers to find more varied or perhaps more unique views. These can provide useful ideas for your own content as well.

Questions For Content

Chapter 4 – Seven Methods You Can Use To Generate Fresh Content From Question and Answer Sites

Useful Methods

In this chapter, I'm going to show you seven methods you can use to generate fresh content using Question and Answer sites. My preference is to work with Quora.com, so I'm going to use that for the examples, but you can work with Yahoo! Answers or any other sites of your choice for this.

Once you have accounts set up on the sites, it's relatively easy to use them for producing content and to inspire your own content creation.

I've come up with a variety of seven ways that work well for using question sites to produce contents. I'm going to share these methods with you now.

Question Site Method #1 – Scrape The Content

The first method I've identified, and I will note straight out that I don't necessarily recommend this one but I'm including it for completeness, is to scrape the content. What that means is you're just going to take the content which is on the site already and put it on your own site.

Now, that may not be appropriate because you may not want to position yourself as a type of person who will use content from elsewhere. But it is allowed by some sites. This includes Quora. Of the various Terms of Service on the site, which I encourage you to read fully if you plan to do this, the ones that stood out to me are the content may not be modified, which means if you take a question and answer, you just have to post them as is. You can't change the questions or answers, you can't correct the spellings, you can't add new words that weren't there and you can't take words out. They've got to be unmodified.

You also have to make sure the author allows this. It's an opt out system, so by default, you're fine. Generally, if someone has opted out of making their content reusable, there will be a note with a post or a badge displayed against it. It's quite rare but you need to check this.

Perhaps the biggest downside for this is you have to provide a link back to the post, the question, the answers on Quora and that may be sending traffic away from your site. So you need to decide whether scraping the content is that valuable to you because for the reasons I discussed earlier in the book about having duplicate content, then Google will have to decide whether to send people to the original site or whether to send it to your site.

Unless you can add a lot to the scraped content, for instance you include that then you include your own opinion on the topic, then scraped content may be of limited value for legitimate sites you're building up for long term profit.

Question Site Method #2 – Use The Site For Ideas

The second method I'm suggesting is for you to use the site for idea. This is generally a great way to get content. It's something I'd recommend. It's to go and do a search on Quora and just to type in keywords related to your niche and see what comes back. If you scan through the results, you're going to get some ideas popping up in front of you.

Now, there's also a way to do this intelligently and strategically and that's to subscribe to the different topics. When you sign up to Quora, you have to say what areas you consider yourself to be an expert in or what areas you're interested in finding out more about. If you choose those areas of expertise then you will get these appearing in your feed on Quora and you can then read this and look and see what topic ideas stand out to you.

It's really just a case of scanning through. You know what appeals to your readership. You know what niche you're in. You know what the kind of keywords to look out for and as soon as you've seen the topics, use those as a basis for an article. Just go ahead and think up your own answer which you feel will match the kind of topics you're seeing because those are real life questions other people are interested in finding out the answers for.

Question Site Method #3 – Use The Site To Compile Content

Way number three is to use the site in the compilation of content. This works well particularly if you find a question which is a few months old because then there will be a large number of answers available for it. The more answers you get, the more opinions you have, the more different ideas you have, starting points for your own original piece of content. So you're really looking for something with at least five answers. You may get away with only having four answers if there's enough detail to them but I think that five answers is a good starting point.

You need to use these questions and the answers as a research source, so you only have to go to a single location, and then you write your own article based on combining together the different opinions, solutions and answers given, restructuring them in an original way and most importantly, you write everything in your own words. In that way, you're using the question site purely as a research source.

The original process of compiling this and using your own words means that this doesn't qualify as duplicate content because it's original content and it also doesn't qualify as plagiarism because you're providing an original interpretation of that data.   That's an excellent way to cut down your research time because all the answers you need there are in one place.

Question Site Method #4 – Use The Site For Ideas And Content

If you can combine together methods two and three, you have a really good way to generate your own fresh content.

This means that you will use the site for both ideas and for content and what that means is you just look at your feeds on the site and you find the topics that stand out to you because they're the ones you think people are interested in, and then you look at the answers as well and you combine them together in an original research form to meet the needs of your audience.

You have the kind of content that you need then produced in a single pass by using the question site. I think that you should be considering this as one of your key takeaways from this book. You need to be using the site for both ideas and content. This is one of my favourite methods for producing content that's of high quality for blogs and sites.

Question Site Method #5 – Outsource Content Production

Here's more of an advanced method, which works well if you're cash rich and time poor.

Sometimes, you just won't be in a position to create all of the content you need for yourself. There just aren't enough hours in the day.

If this is the case, you can look to outsource the content production using the question sites. Essentially, this just means that you're going to teach a third party to compile the content on your behalf. They're going to use the question sites in exactly the same way.

Because you're sending these people to the question sites, you know they're starting off with interesting content and the kind of questions other people want to have answered and generally, because of the way that Quora allows people to indicate their expertise and to classify their role, then you know you're starting off with answers that have some value to them, particularly if you look at the answers the community has voted to the top.

Now, you can't assume your outsourcing worker, regardless of how you found them, whether it's on a site like oDesk or an often less-expensive site like Fiverr.com, will know how to use these question sites so you do need to show them this process yourself. One good way to do that is just to provide them a video showing a walkthrough of what you want to be done. But this potentially a wise time versus money decision because if you can find somebody whose hourly rate is well below yours but can still produce good quality content which engages your readership then why not use them rather than doing this difficult and time consuming task for yourself?

Question Site Method #6 – Ask Questions Directly On The Site

What about if you've got an idea of the kind of questions people in your niche want to know but maybe you're not that confident about the answers? Maybe it's not a niche that you're in because you're an expert but one because you see the money making potential. Then how do you collect together appropriate content?

In that case, you ask the questions yourself. That's a perfectly legitimate use of the site and then you use the research provided by the multiple answers given in order to pull together your own articles and your own posts or perhaps your video content, depending on the way you process this.

That can be a good technique for many reasons, because somewhere on your profile, you're likely to provide a link to this site and that has then a relationship between your Quora profile and your site and the type of questions you're asking. It shows all these links together, that this niche is one in which you should be taken seriously.

You probably need to wait a few days, particularly if you ask the kind of question where there are many knowledgeable people, in order to collect things. If you do want to speed this up, of course you can ask more than one question at once. You can also provide answers to some questions where you do have an opinion, because that does demonstrate expertise as well and that's another advance tactic you should be considering. But do ask questions yourself when you need more content.

Question Site Method #7 – Ask For <u>Question Ideas</u> On The Question Site

The final method is to not just to use the question site to provide answers but it's also to use that site to provide ideas for questions.

All you do for this is you go on the site and pose questions and see what answers come back.

Here are some starter questions you could tailor to your niche and use:

- "Can you tell me what the biggest questions are that people have with blank?"
- "What would you rate the biggest questions in the last six months to be?"
- "What changes have there been in this area which need questions to be addressed?"
- "If you were to tell a beginner ten different questions in this niche, what would they be?"

You need to ask people to contribute their own ideas and to share them.

Once you've started to receive answers (in the form of questions), you can take those questions and you can combine them with some of the earlier ways.

The easiest way would be to just post the question verbatim on the site. Just post it, leave it for a while and see what the answers are that come back. Then generate your own original content based on those answers.

Often though, you might find that the question is one you can answer yourself, or at least provide your own opinion on. If so, there's no need to go through the extra stage of posing that question again. You can just go ahead and write a new article yourself, whether it's based on facts or whether it's opinion-based.

If you do this, you've got a very good use of your time because you're taking advantage of the power of the crowd, those people there who do want to contribute. There are a lot of people out there who just enjoy showing what they know and providing information. That's a whole process which powers massive communities like Wikipedia.

Combining The Seven Techniques

In this chapter, I've shown you seven techniques which can be very powerful when you need to generate content.

You may not want to use all of them, but when you do, you can also generate some really original content and ideas that help to pull people to your site. I recommend that you try combining several of these ideas when you can.

In the next chapter, I'm going to show you a case study about how you can use a question site to generate your own original content.

Chapter 5 – A Case Study Using A Question Site To Generate Original Content

Case Study

In this chapter, I'm going to show you an example of how you can compile a fresh piece of content using some of these methods I outlined in Chapter 4.

This case study is based on one of the techniques I would use if I wanted to enter a new niche and to generate high quality content quickly.

To tie in with the theme of the book, I'm going to base the case study largely around **content strategy**. That's an important area now for online businesses and a niche you could enter, set up a business and really make some traction. If you're a freelance writer, this is also a great niche in which you can demonstrate your own expertise in the area.

Now, of course I know a fair amount about content strategy in general, but to make this into a fair case study, I'm going to choose an example question more at the outliers of my knowledge.

A Real Life Case Study Question

Here's the question I've selected as the basis for this case study.

What are the best ways to find a great writer for a startup?

I've selected this question deliberately because it looked interesting on a quick look through the feed of questions available. Having an interest in a question is a great way to stay motivated when writing about it.

It's also an area I don't know all that much about. I know a fair amount about content strategy and I have some experience with startup companies, but I've never really considered combining the two together, or how to get the best writers for that type of environment.

This is definitely a real life situation too.

I could probably make a reasonable stab at answering this question and sharing some opinions, but the expert knowledge from Quora is of so much value here.

The other reason this question appealed to me, for the purpose of demonstrating a viable solution for this book, is that the question had six answers to it. That's a manageable number.

Take a look at Figure 3 and you can see what the whole page on Quora looks like with all six answers. Now, there's rather too much information for a single book page, but I'll go into more of the detail later in the chapter. This is just to give you an idea about the volume of information you have to work with.

Questions For Content

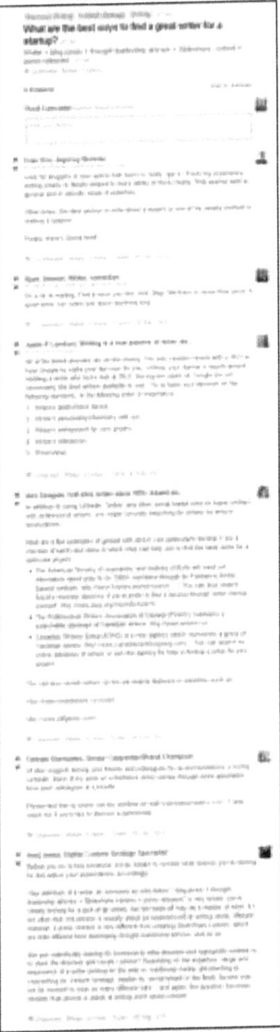

Figure 3 - Case Study Question With Answers On Quora

Here are some areas it's worth paying attention to in Figure 3.

You can see that, out of the six answers, the answer towards the top is the one that's received the highest number of votes from other Quora readers. The answer at the bottom is the one that's received the fewest votes. Now, it may not necessarily be the worst possible answer. It may just be that's the newest answer and people haven't commented on it yet.

Regarding the answers themselves, what you have is a manageable number there. They all look like reasonable quality answers to. There's a bit of substance to all of the answers and certainly you can read through them all.

If you add it all up, there's easily 1,000 words of content there that you could repurpose. You can create a good blog post with 200 or 300 words. You can create a longer article which is more of a feature with between 400 and 600 words. You could also use the content ideas to form a feature video.

What all of this means is that you don't need to use much of the ideas from the answers in one go. If you're smart about it, you can take this single article and form it into multiple blog posts, articles, videos and other pieces of content. That's a valuable strategic way to work with content.

Now, let's drill down into this particular question in a bit more detail.

Figure 4 shows the question as it's posted on the site.

What are the best ways to find a great writer for a startup? *Edit*
Writer = blog posts + thought leadership articles + Slideshare content + press releases. *Edit*

Figure 4 - Case Study Question And Clarification On Quora

As well as the raw question, Figure 4 also provides a further level of clarification about what the person asking the question was hoping to get from the answer they received. That's line below the original question.

That means that the question asks:

> "What are the best ways to find a great writer for a start-up?"

The additional clarification adds:

> "Writer = blog posts + thought leadership articles + slide share content + press releases."

Overall, that's rather a varied request. In many ways, that's good, as it's suitable for prompting a wide selection of answers.

Article Titles Ideas From The Case Study Question

Even without reading through the answers, you can get some ideas for article titles just by looking at the content and the associated additional clarification detail.

It's useful to think about this early on in the process of looking at the question and answers. The titles you've come up with will help you to decide how to focus when you read the answers.

If you don't have any immediate ideas for titles, this might also be an indication that this particular question isn't a good one for you.

You can always review the titles you've proposed as you go further through the process of reading the different answers to. This one is just a starting point.

Here are three quick content title ideas I came up with when reading through this question:

- Finding The Perfect Writer For A Startup Business

- Outsourcing Content Creation For Your Startup Business

- Three Mistakes To Avoid When Outsourcing Content Creation For Your Startup Business

You might notice I've automatically focused two of these questions on the content side rather than the writer side. I only realised in hindsight when I was editing this book that I'd done that, but it just shows how your own work is automatically tailored towards your interests.

It does also mean that you could write all three of these pieces of content without needing to repeat yourself too much. This is valuable, as you're getting more content using a single question as your source.

I also want to focus in a bit on the final suggested title, which is looking for "three mistakes". There's a bit of reverse psychology there, as people reading articles always like to know what's gone wrong for other people. It's a hook to draw them in. To me, that title works really well.

If you prefer to present this as a positive, you could just as easily write about "Three Factors to Look Out for when Outsourcing Content Creation for Your Start-Up Business".

I also really like the numeric model. Putting a number in your content title makes this much easier to create and saves you running off course. You might notice that I've used exactly that technique throughout the book, including in Chapter 4, which I based around seven methods.

For the case study, you could take the second suggest title and use this technique to make this into a numbered process. One title that might then work is "Outsourcing Content Creation for Your Start-Up Business in Five Steps".

Researching Content For The Title Ideas

Whether you already have title ideas, or whether you're going to generate these as you read, the next stage involves research. When you do this, you can generate relevant content in the level of detail you prefer.

What you do now is quite simple. You just systematically work through the answers from the start to the end. In this case, there are only six answers, so I'm going to try and grab some ideas from all of these. If there are a much longer number of answers to choose between, you might be more selective, just looking at the first few answers, then skim reading the rest to see if there are any zany ideas that stick out that you'd like to make use of.

It also helps to have a title to base the research around.

> I'm going to base my research around my preferred title of *"Three Mistakes To Avoid When Outsourcing Content Creation For Your Startup Business"*.

There would be nothing to stop you making notes and collecting ideas for multiple titles at the same time.

I'm going to use each of the answers to generate two or three short bullet point style ideas, bearing in mind that the ideas will likely start to overlap as we go through the answers. Then, I'm going to combine them together at the end to see what we have.

I'll discuss my thought process in a bit more detail for the early answers. For the latter ones, I'll condense this a bit as I hope you'll soon get the idea. It's easy to get "in the zone" once you've looked at a few questions and the associated sets of answers.

Case Study Answer #1

Figure 5 shows the first answer, from Eran Dror, who has self-classified himself as an aspiring novelist.

This is the highest rated answer, but it is only two votes, so it's not a massive number. That's another reason I would expect to find something useful in all of the answers to this question.

Eran Dror, Aspiring Novelist
2 votes by Matthew Edward and Mary C Long

Look for bloggers in your space that seem to really "get it." From my experience, writing clearly is deeply related to one's ability to think clearly. That applies both in general and in specific areas of expertise.

Often times, the best person to write about a project is one of the people involved in making it happen.

Finally, there's Quora itself.

Figure 5 - Case Study Answer #1

Eron says "Look for bloggers in your space that seem to really get it. From my experience, writing clearly is deeply related to one's ability to think clearly. That applies both in general and in specific areas of expertise." Oftentimes, the best person to write about a project is one of the people involved in making it happen. Finally, there's Quora itself" – which is an interesting hint at the bottom, that you could use that very site – "to find your writers because you can see what their writing style is like and how qualified they are."

The ideas that stand out to me are first of all to employ quality bloggers, in other words "the people in the space that get it". Use a project team – to me, that's an excellent idea because these people are working day in, day out for this small start-up business and they will know the area, they will know what the frustrations are, they'll know who they're aiming it at as well. I'm going to record the idea to use Quora as well. It's what we're working with in this book and it doesn't hurt to have a further plug.

Summary Of Ideas From Case Study Answer #1

- Employ quality bloggers
- Use the project team
- Use Quora

Case Study Answer #2

Figure 6 shows the second answer, which comes courtesy of Ryan Skinner.

Figure 6 - Case Study Answer #2

I'm going to summarise the ideas I've picked up from Figure 6. First of all, Ryan says that you should read around and find people you like because a lot of having a good site is about getting somebody whose style appeals to you. Equally importantly, you need to be willing to pay because you want the very best people who are going to cost more money.

In my mind, there's more than one way to pay because it could be for a small start-up business financially but it could also be longer term in terms of telling them about the contacts they'll make, the connections, perhaps the share options. There's more than one way to pay but turning that on its head, don't go cheap because this content is there forever and that's one reason why as part of *Questions For Content* overall that I'm encouraging you to produce your own content, where you can.

Summary Of Ideas From Case Study Answer #2

- Read and find people you like
- Be willing to pay for the best people

Case Study Answer #3

Figure 7 shows the third ranked answer, from Justin P Lambert, who says that he's a passionate write. This one has clearly been written after a few other answers were already on the site.

Justin P Lambert, Writing is a true passion of mine, an...
1 vote by Ann Douglas

All of the above answers are on the money. The only caution I would add is NOT to trust Google to make your decision for you. Unless your startup is based around needing a writer who kicks butt at SEO, the top ten spots on Google are not necessarily the best writers available to you. Try to base your decision on the following elements, in the following order of importance:

1. Writer's ability/track record
2. Writer's personality/chemistry with you
3. Writer's enthusiasm for your project
4. Writer's references
5. Price/Value

Figure 7 - Case Study Answer #3

Justin has ranked five different factors in what he feels are the most important. Of course, you may not agree with him. You don't have to rank things in the same way because it's your own content you're producing. But you can certainly take from that even without looking at the details that you need to identify and order your priorities. You may say this is a standard thing but people still need to be reminded of this when they read articles and they look at your own answer to these problems.

It's that you shouldn't rely on SEO writers (SEO stands for Search Engine Optimisation). It's people who write purely to trick Google and to show them they've used keywords over and over again. I think that's valid because in my mind, a lot of people who write purely for Search Engine Optimisation are turning out very quick, cheap, low quality content and it's not going to meet the needs that I discussed in Chapter 2 of the book, about the content needing to be inspiring and engaging. You want to go beyond that.

The third idea we'll take from here is that we should consider the track record of the writer. What have they done before? Can they show you the type of sites they've written for? There may be some confidentiality issues. If they have their own blog which they can show, what have they done? Have they worked well for this particular area with other sort of businesses and improved their visitors, improved the engagement on the site and improved the stick rate?

So those are three more great ideas.

Summary Of Ideas From Case Study Answer #3

- Identify and order your priorities
- Don't rely on SEO writers for startups
- Consider the track record of the writer

Case Study Answer #4

Figure 8 shows the next answer. This was a longer answer than some of the others, so I've cut this down slightly to fit in the book and left the highlights that I'm going to work with.

Ann Douglas, Full-time writer since 1992. Award-wi...

In addition to using LinkedIn, Twitter, and other social media sites to make contact with professional writers, you might consider searching for writers via writers' associations.

Here are a few examples of groups with which I am particularly familiar (I am a member of each) and ways in which they can help you to find the ideal writer for a particular project.

- The American Society of Journalists and Authors (ASJA) will send out

You can also recruit writers via the job boards featured on websites such as

http://www.mediabistro.com/jobli...

http://www.jeffgaulin.com/

Figure 8 - Case Study Answer #4

Ann Douglas talks a lot about social media and mentions the different sites used. These are places like LinkedIn for professional social media, as well as Twitter. She also talks about using these to contact the writers. That's a smart move because quite often people's contact details aren't as clearly available as you might like, particularly when it's somebody who's not solely a writer but they also work mainly for themselves or do other things as well. Then you can attract some high quality freelance writers who wouldn't otherwise be available for you.

It's also identified that there are whole groups of freelance writers. There are online communities where they hang out and there are societies. One example on there is the American Society of Journalists and Authors.

Ann also suggests using online job sites to find them and again, there are some examples provided. These job boards, people are actively looking for work. This means that, chances are they'll likely be receptive to whatever deal you want to put to them.

Summary Of Ideas From Case Study Answer #4

- Contact writers through social media
- Use groups of freelance writers
- Use online job sites

Case Study Answer #5

Answer number five comes from Celeste Giampetro, who presents herself as a senior copywriter. There's a good use of branding in this answer, as well as a link to content her if you'd like to work with her. Just another way you can use Quora if you're smart about it.

Celeste Giampetro, Senior Copywriter/Brand Champion

I'd also suggest asking your friends and colleagues for recommendations or trying LinkedIn. Most of my work as a freelance writer comes through leads generated from past colleagues or LinkedIn.

Please feel free to check out my portfolio as well (celestegiampetro.com) and reach out if you'd like to discuss a partnership.

Figure 9 - Case Study Answer #5

What kind of ideas have we got from Celeste? First of all, to ask friends and colleagues. I think recommendations of writers is really important because if somebody has a writer but they don't have enough work to keep them going all the time then they may be interested in helping you to use them as well.

You could also, of course, ask your friends and colleagues to be the writers if they're looking to make a little extra money, although often working with friends can be a difficult process, so perhaps best avoid it.

There's also a suggestion of using LinkedIn. I've added that here because it's an important part of answer number five but it overlaps as well with one of the previous answers, so this will be discounted when we summarise later on. This isn't because the answer isn't valid. If anything, you might want to consider it as more valid, as the same point has been repeated by several people.

Summary Of Ideas From Case Study Answer #5

- Ask friends and colleagues
- Use LinkedIn

Case Study Answer #6

The final answer is shown in Figure 10, which comes from Heej Jones.

Heej Jones, Digital Content Strategy Specialist

Before you try to hire someone, it'd be helpful to cement what exactly you're looking for and adjust your expectations accordingly.

Your definition of a writer as someone as who writes " blog posts + thought leadership articles + Slideshare content + press releases" is very broad; you're clearly looking for a jack of all trades, but the trade-off may be a master of none. It's not often that one person is equally adept (or experienced) at writing vastly different material; a press release is very different from creating SlideShare content, which are both different from developing thought leadership articles, and so on.

Are you realistically looking for someone to take direction and regurgitate content or to steer the direction and create content? Depending on the expertise, range and experience of a writer (writing for the web vs. traditional media; ghostwriting or copywriting vs. content strategy, newbie vs. senior/expert in the field), he/she may not be inclined to wear so many different hats -- and again, the question becomes whether that person is adept at writing such varied content.

Figure 10 - Case Study Answer #6

Heej talks about cementing what you're looking for and clarifying your expectations of the writer. That's really important because the original question seems to suggest that somebody would be an expert in all very different areas – blog posts, thought leadership articles, SlideShare content (that's online slideshows, rather like presentations in PowerPoint) and press releases.

That may not be a good move.

An alternative would be to use more than one writer. For instance, you could hire four good writers, pay them for a quarter of the time each and you end up with higher quality work at the end.

I like the phrase "Jack of all trades" which is included there. It's often said "If you're a Jack of all trades, you're a master of none". I don't know if that is always completely true. Just thinking about myself, there are a lot of things that I can do well, particularly in relation to the marketing area. I can then combine them all together. By the same token there are things that I know I am awful at. I'm not so great at graphical work, so for me it would be more advantageous to outsource this then to spend all the time attempting to make graphics myself.

If you find one person who's really good at SlideShare content, which could really just mean making and converting Power-Point presentations, then one person who's really good at press releases and then different people for all the different content production niches, you've probably got a much better overall solution.

Summary Of Ideas From Case Study Answer #6

- Clarify expectations of the writer
- Use more than one writer
- Avoid a "jack of all trades"

15 Points Of Value From The Case Studies Answers

To quickly summarise the different ideas, combining them together and removing the duplicate reference to LinkedIn, gives us the following list:

1. Employ quality bloggers
2. Use the project team
3. Use Quora
4. Read and find people you like
5. Be willing to pay for the best people
6. Identify and order your priorities
7. Don't rely on SEO writers for startups
8. Consider the track record of the writer
9. Contact writers through social media and LinkedIn
10. Use groups of freelance writers
11. Use online job sites
12. Ask friends and colleagues
13. Clarify expectations of the writer
14. Use more than one writer
15. Avoid a "jack of all trades"

You might want to sort and prioritise these in some way, I've chosen not to.

I've also deliberately not referred back to the original sources. To me, these are being used for idea generation, but the intention isn't to go back and take content from the original answers given by the different Quora contributors.

Many of these points have enough value to them where you could create a whole piece of content. I'm going to stick with the three point article format. There are a lot of benefits to that format. One is that I can write a short blog post without needing to do any further research or to think about this for too long.

You can also use these 15 points to form the basis of many articles, just by choosing three different points for each article. If you just use each point once, that's five articles right there. You could also reuse points more than once, as the context will change as you put these into different articles.

Of course, you can also turn the positive points on their head and use these as the basis for the "you should not do this" style of article.

Putting all of those considerations together, here's an outline for an article I could write based on the content researched from Quora.

Example Article Structure Based On The Case Study

Here is the type of structure I would work with when writing a fresh and original article, based on the ideas I've found from other people.

I've picked out three of the ideas which I think work really well in the "mistake" format and which I can write about relatively easily.

Three Mistakes To Avoid When Outsourcing Content Creation For Your Startup Business

Example Article Structure

- Why your startup business needs content
- Mistake #1 – Hiring a single writer who can't handle all areas of the business
- Mistake #2 – Not asking the project team to contribute based on their own expertise
- Mistake #3 – Hiring a writer who is SEO focused

Questions For Content

- Recommendations

This type of structure makes it incredibly easy to put together an interesting 500 word article. You just take the five bullet points and write around 100 words for each of them.

First of all, I would give a brief introduction about why your start-up business needs content and you've got enough there to write it. I would mention similar challenges to the ones I've discussed earlier in this chapter.

After the introduction, I'd just discuss each of the mistakes in turn.

Mistake number one that stood out to me is hiring a single writer who can't handle all areas of business. You can flesh that section out by presenting the alternative, which is to either hire the writer carefully, or to use multiple writers.

Mistake number two is not asking the project team to contribute based on their own expertise. Particularly for a technical-type project, the team could easily be the best people because of the technical knowledge needed. If you find an external representative, it's much harder to guarantee that that person has the correct level of technical knowledge. The team will also want to feel that they're involved. Often the people working in these smaller start-ups, in my opinion, like to get themselves known and advertise. One reason that they do this is just in case a start-up doesn't work out so they've got future job prospects from the time and effort they've put in.

Mistake number three is hiring a writer who is purely focused on Search Engine Optimisation. You can relate that to the fact this writer is probably cheap, they're just looking to make sure that certain keywords are used multiple times within an article. They're not going to turn out the engaging content you want.

Putting those mistakes together, you already have an article which is both interesting and useful.

You still need to conclude the article in a sensible way, ideally with a call to action. You could conclude that with recommendations about what type of person would be best to hire instead.

It may well be that this is the type of article you write if you're a freelance writer looking to get hired yourself. In this case, the call to action would be for someone to hire you. You've already demonstrated that you can write interesting content based on what's in the article.

If, instead, you're looking to sell a product to your visitor, you might instead direct them through an affiliate link to a book on Amazon that you'll receive a commission for, or to a training course that already exists.

Importantly, you have provided a visitor who has arrived from Google or another search engines with the kind of information they wanted.   They found out about mistakes when outsourcing content creation as promised. Even if they were looking for what they should do instead, you've also covered that in your article.

I hope you can see how you could take that structure and easily get an interesting 500 word article from it. You just need to write 100 words on each of those different varied points.

If you need a shorter article, you could just reduce the amount of time you spend talking about each of these points. To get a 300 word article, you'd just cover 60 words for each of these sections.

To get a longer article, you could write more for each of these sections, or just cover more points. For instance, you could write about five or seven mistakes instead of three mistakes.

Three Mistakes To Avoid When Outsourcing Content Creation For Your Startup Business

The Finished Article

Here is an article I wrote based on these ideas. It took me about 10 minutes, but you can speed up by writing several articles together while the ideas are fresh in your mind.

You can also find this article on my blog at http://thomlancaster.com.

Three Mistakes To Avoid When Outsourcing Content Creation For Your Startup Business

If you've launched a new business, whether you're an individual, working with partners, or with a small team, you're going to need content to promote your business. By content, I mean the articles you post on your blog, the videos you release and all the positive messaging you put out there to make sure that potential customers know about you and your brand.

But, what do you do if you're too busy to create all of this high quality content for yourself? Well then, you can outsource the content creation and hire someone to create it for you. But if you're not done this before, you might make mistakes. I've picked out three mistakes which you should avoid when you're outsourcing content for your startup business.

Mistake #1 – Hiring a single writer who can't handle all areas of the business

There are a lot of excellent writers out there, but just because someone sends you their writing samples about dog food and proves that they can write, this doesn't mean that they can also write about the field you're in. Or, they might be able to write about the business side of your field, but not the more technical side. You need to choose a writer carefully, really interview and speak to them and check the right familiarity necessary, or at least can research effectively as needed. If this doesn't work for you, why not think about hiring a team of writers instead? They can be employed on a part time or freelance basis and each just concentrate on the areas they're good at.

Mistake #2 – Not asking the project team to contribute based on their own expertise

If you're working in a team, you already have the resources on hand to create good content. You have access to people who are passionate about the project you're working on together being successful. You have people who are already knowledgeable about the area. Why not ask them and see if they want to contribute or if they have great ideas for themselves? You could give them some guidance about the type of content you want, or even encourage them to contribute articles that are more technically rich. Your team members also get the benefit of promoting themselves through their content, which can help them to feel more valued.

Mistake #3 – Hiring a writer who is SEO focused

One of the biggest problems I've seen with writers is that a lot of them have just been taught to be Search Engine Optimisation (SEO) focused. That means they concentrate more on working certain key terms into the articles they're writing rather than making sure it reads well and interests and engages your site visitors. That's not good, as poor quality content that is designed more for computers than humans will just put off your potential customers. The search engines, such as Google, have also got wise to this trick. Hire people who have proven writing ability and you'll go a lot further.

Avoid These Mistakes

I recommend that you take care to avoid these three mistakes with your growing business. Make sure that you have the right team of writers in place who can cover all aspects of business and produce fresh content for it. Try and involve your project team as well. They can concentrate content directly and this may complement the content produced by your writing team well. Whoever you hire, make sure that they are writing for the benefit of readers, by providing excellent and insightful content, rather than for machines. That will help more people to see your content and appreciate your brand and you'll get much more value from the content you've had produced.

Now, quite frankly this isn't the best article I've ever written, but it's good enough and really this is just there to give you a flavor of how to write the final content.

You may also notice I've got over the word count and not divided everything evenly up into 100 word sections. That's fine, as that's realistic and true to life. There are 616 words there, including the section headings which help to break this up. I could easily have written 200 or so words more without having to think too much. That's all fine as long content is in demand right now.

Here's what the start of the article looks like on my blog:

Three Mistakes To Avoid When Outsourcing Content Creation For Your Startup Business

 Friday, March 16th, 2018 at 9:54 am   Edit

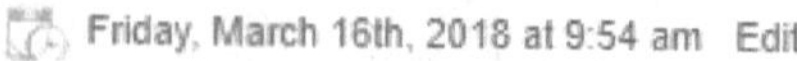

Like   Sign Up to see what your friends like.   Tweet

If you've launched a new business, whether you're an individual, working with partners, or with a small team, **you're going to need content to promote your business**. By content, I mean the articles you post on your blog, the videos you release and all the positive messaging you put out there to make sure that potential customers know about you and your brand.

But, what do you do if you're too busy to create all of this high quality content for yourself? Well then, you can outsource the content creation and hire someone to create it for you. But if you're not done this before, you might make mistakes. I've picked out three mistakes which you should avoid when you're outsourcing content for your startup business.

Mistake #1 – Hiring a single writer who can't handle all areas of the business

There are a lot of excellent writers out there, but just because someone sends you their writing samples about dog food and proves that they can write, this doesn't mean that they can also write about the field you're in.

Case Study Summary

Putting all of these ideas together, you have a really powerful system for quickly generating fresh and interesting content. This will even work for areas that you don't know much about.

To attempt to systemise this, you can think about the following process:

1. Identify a question on Quora that you'd like fresh content on
    - Think about a manageable number of answers for this area
2. Write down some possible titles for content articles that you could generate based on the question
    - Numeric focused answers, such as "three steps" or "three mistakes" work well
3. Read through the first few answers and note the key ideas as bullet points
    - If there are a lot of answers, you can also skim read the later ones
4. Combine the key ideas you've identified into a single list, removing the duplicates
5. Select and order the ideas to give you a structure for your article

- You can get structures for multiple articles from a single set of ideas
- You can also create your content to different lengths and in multiple formats

6. Create your fresh, original and engaging content

The brilliance of the *Questions For Content* system is that much of the hard work of coming up with ideas is already done for you. You're benefitting from crowdsourced ideas from a whole host of interesting people. These ideas are already sorted and put into priority order.

With this system and practice, you could easily generate five short fresh articles on a new subject in an hour or two.

Chapter 6 – Your Fast Action Plan For Content Production Using The *Questions For Content* System

Fast Action Plan

I want to conclude *Questions For Content* by providing you with an action plan so that you can get started with writing and producing your own high quality content quickly. I'm going to base the action plan around Quora, as I think it's the best site for this type of question-based research.

The most important thing you have to do is join the site. You have to fill in your profile, even if you use Facebook registration. You have to choose the areas of expertise that you have but these really should be the areas in which you need content, because these are the topics your sites are on in which you're attempting to use this site for. If you miss anything, the search is great there.

I then recommend you go straight in and you follow the process that I've overviewed in this book to choose a question and to compile the main points made by the contributors. You can just do this on a scrap of paper. I like to open a Notepad file on the computer and just write a few words in there. You can even copy and paste short segments but I prefer to write things straight in my own words, then there's no chance of ever accidentally using the original source documents because you haven't got that there to use.

Then take all those points, arrange them in an order that works for you and write at least one original piece of content for your site or blog or prepare this as a video, whatever method you use which works for your own site or blog. Ideally, while you're at it, I recommend that you make several pieces of content because it's best to do that while you're in the mood and while you've got these ideas. By doing that, you can even enter an area you know nothing about and which you've not been involved with before.

Content Is Vital For Your Online Prosperity

I hope that I've stressed this enough in the book for you, but having a supply of high quality content is absolutely essential if you want to make a name online for yourself or your online business. I hope that you understand the reasons why you need all of this from *Questions For Content*.

You really can use these question sites to speed up the process of creating high quality content. I've demonstrated that in this book. I've provided you with seven ways you can use that but the most important one is quite simply to go on Quora, browse through the questions, use the search, find areas you're interested in with several answers and then to use this as a massive research source to put together interesting articles for your site and blogs.

If you put all that together, you get what I feel is a perfect content creation strategy that pulls together the difficulties of research and exploring a new area, and allows you to use your own writing expertise or perhaps those of your outsourcing team, to produce high quality, engaging content.

If you were so inclined, you could even generate the content to fill a whole book (like this one) with the *Questions For Content* strategy.

Do please visit my online site and blog if you want to find out more about my own content and the areas that I'm interested in.

You can find out more about me at http://thomlancaster.com.

Thanks for taking reading *Questions For Content*. Do go ahead and use Quora and put together your own high quality posts and articles.

Questions For Content

Questions For Content